WALT DISNEY ANIMATION STUDIOS

The Archive Series

LAYOUT & BACKGROUND

DISNEY EDITIONS

NEW YORK

PREVIOUS SPREAD: **BAMBI** 1942

Also from

Walt Disney Animation Studios: The Archive Series

STORY

ANIMATION

DESIGN

For information address Disney Editions, 114 Fifth Avenue, New York, New York 10011-5690.

Printed in Malaysia

First Edition
10 9 8 7 6 5 4 3 2

ISBN 978-1-4231-3866-2
H106-9333-5-12278
This book is printed on a paper from a sustainable source

Designed by Hans Teensma, Impress, Inc.

THE BAND CONCERT 1935

WINTER STORAGE 1949

SETTING THE STAGE

BY JOHN LASSETER

ONE OF THE THINGS Walt Disney did so well was take an audience into the world of a story. Watch any Disney movie, and you'll immediately be carried away to another time and place, whether it's a forest clearing, the cluttered attic of a London townhouse, or King Louie's jungle throne room. (You can also see the same expertise at work in the many lands of Disneyland.) From the start, the artists working on the Disney animated films did an incredible job creating beautiful, detailed, and appealing worlds; worlds you want to be in.

In an animated film, the backgrounds and layouts are what create these worlds. Character design and animation understandably get most of the attention when discussing the art that goes into a film. But it's the carefully designed — and often amazingly beautiful — backgrounds that show us where all the action takes place and help us understand the unspoken rules affecting the characters' behavior by establishing the look and feel and scale of the worlds they navigate.

Layouts are the planning images that help the filmmakers work out the precise details of how an environment will look as a character and the camera moves through it, while backgrounds are the environments that appear

SUSIE, THE LITTLE BLUE COUPE 1952

SNOW WHITE AND
THE SEVEN DWARFS 1937

in the film itself. In classic, hand-drawn animation, backgrounds are individual pieces of art that incorporate all the constant elements of a scene; everything except the characters and the props those characters interact with. Computer-animated films use paintings as well — matte paintings are used to fill in faraway vistas — but since the regular "backgrounds" in these films are really sets composed of many individual elements, we've chosen characteristic stills to represent the backgrounds from these projects. No matter how they've been created, though, the attention to detail and thoughtful planning that go into each environment are the same.

In the best movies, every element works together to support the story. Color, along with music, is one of the most effective ways to communicate the underlying emotion of a scene, and color and lighting can tell you a tremendous amount about the mood of a particular moment. When the color and lighting harmonize with the action and dialogue, they powerfully reinforce what's taking place with the characters. When they're different from the explicit action, they signal change and tension. In every case, the background can tell you the emotion of a scene at a glance.

Backgrounds can also tell you more about a place — and more convincingly — than dialogue ever could. Neverland's caricatured, fantastical settings contrast beautifully with the film's elegant but more serious London,

and perfectly create the feeling of a giant playground where Peter Pan and the Lost Boys would want to stay forever and never grow up. The clever and intricate toys that fill Geppetto's workshop show the incredible care and skill he's put into his craft over the years, while the humble surroundings show us that he's done it not for riches or glory, but for the sake of the work itself.

The genius of these backgrounds is that they do all this work without ever calling attention to themselves or interrupting the flow of the story. They work seamlessly with all the other parts of the film to let you focus on just being with the characters, being in the story.

It's not often that you get the chance to look at a background or layout by itself, and that's a big part of what makes this book such a treat. Being able to take your time with these pieces lets you fully appreciate the level of artistry that goes into them, and understand what an important role they play in the films we love.

Looking through this book I see page after page of places that were as real to me as a kid — and now as a filmmaker — as any I'd ever read or heard about or seen in real life. It's wonderful to finally be able to give them the spotlight they deserve.

John Lasseter

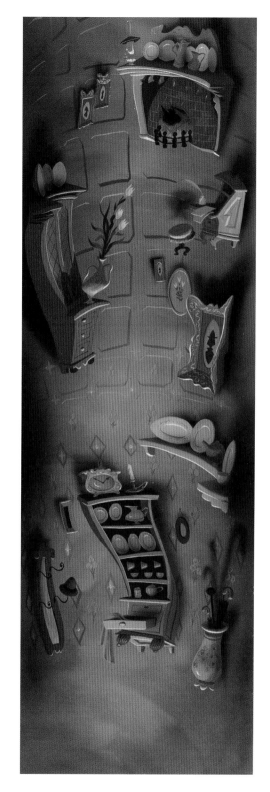

ALICE IN WONDERLAND 1951

FOLLOWING SPREAD: **PLUTO AND THE ARMADILLO** 1943

BRIGHT LIGHTS 1928

THE OPRY HOUSE 1929

SPRINGTIME 1929 AUTUMN 1930

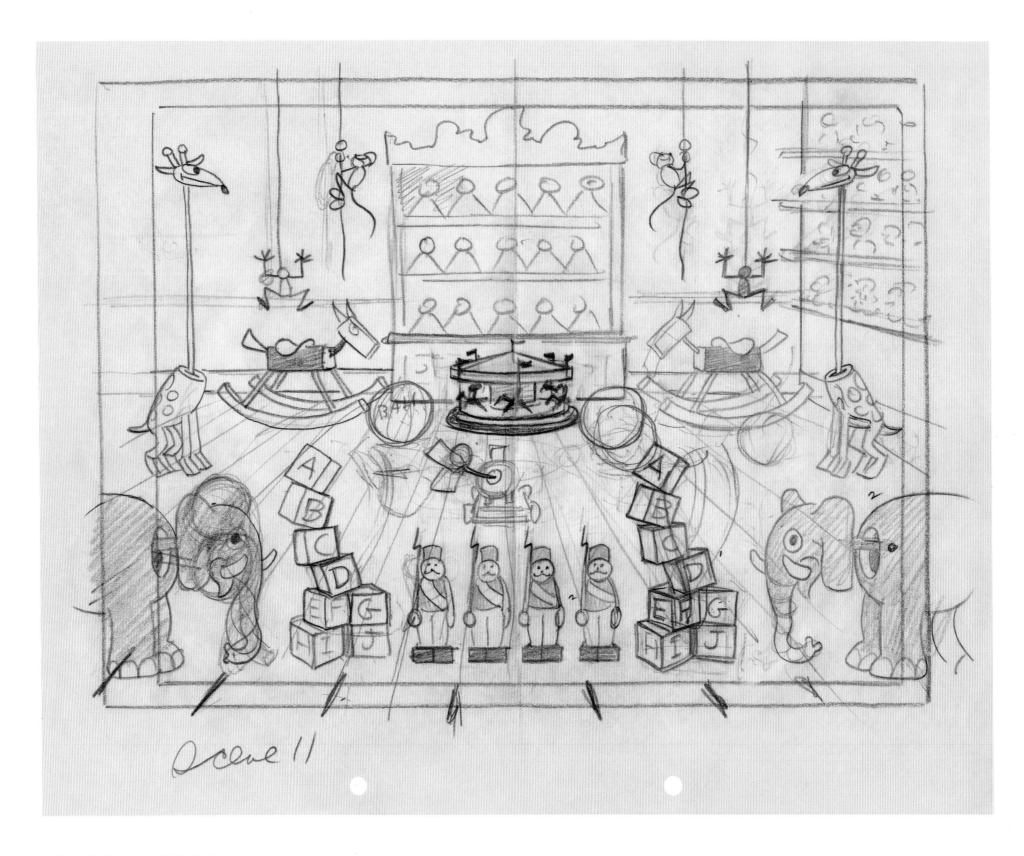

MIDNIGHT IN A TOY SHOP 1930

MOTHER GOOSE MELODIES 1931

THE BARNYARD BROADCAST 1931

LAYOUT & BACKGROUND

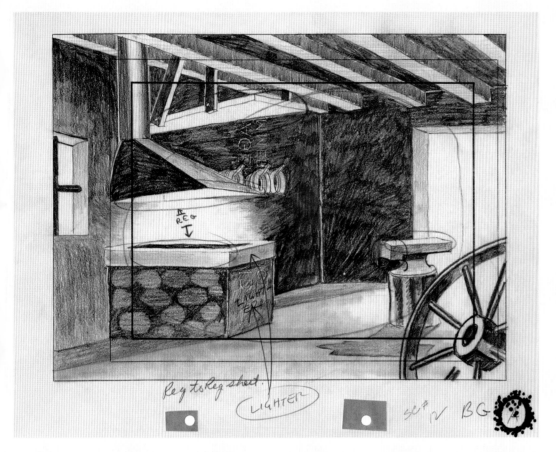

THE FOX HUNT 1931

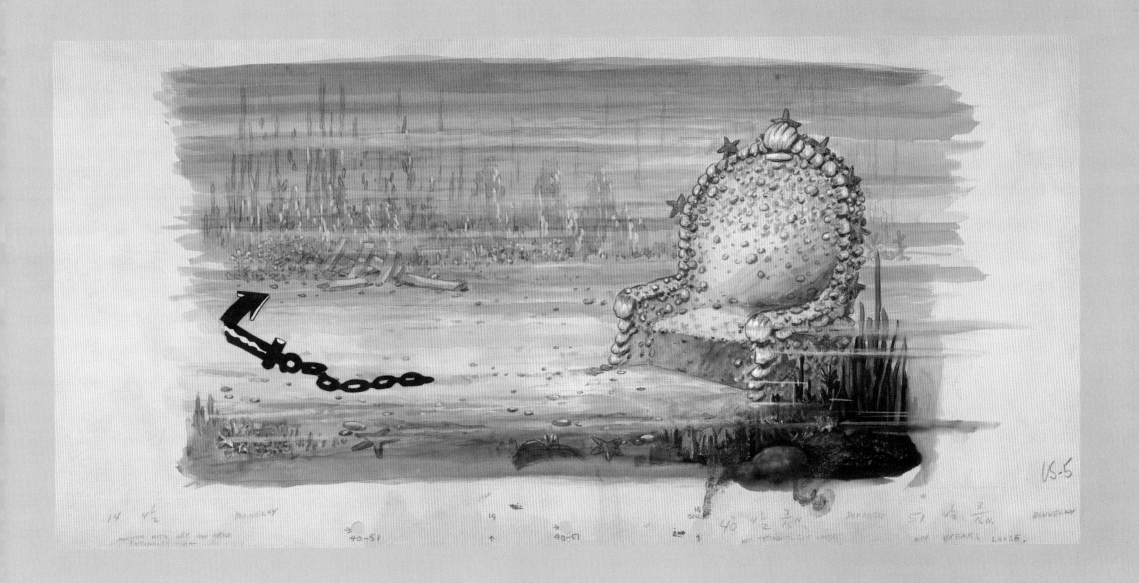

KING NEPTUNE 1932

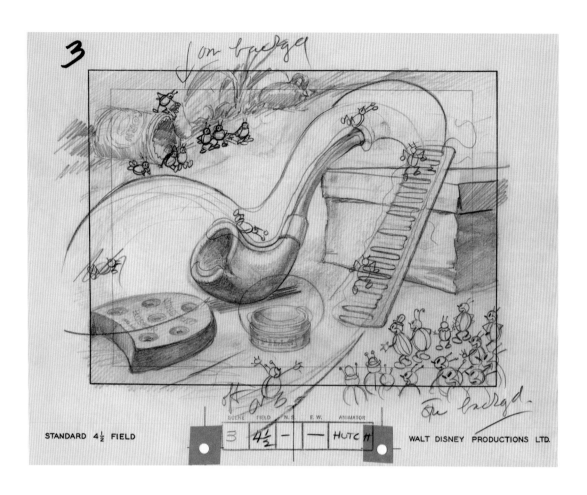

BUGS IN LOVE 1932

YE OLDEN DAYS 1933

PLAYFUL PLUTO 1934

THE WISE LITTLE HEN 1934

US-22 Sc.1 US-22 1 STO 3¼ CY YOUNG '34
WAS USED IN OLD HALLWAY EXHIBIT ANIMATION BUILDING

THE GODDESS OF SPRING 1934

THE GOLDEN TOUCH 1935

PLUTO'S JUDGEMENT DAY 1935

LAYOUT & BACKGROUND

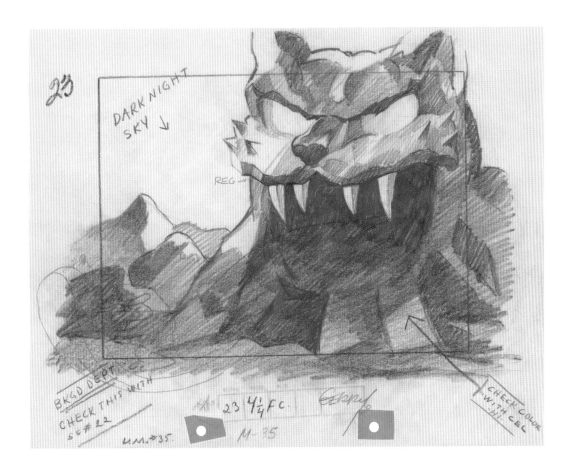

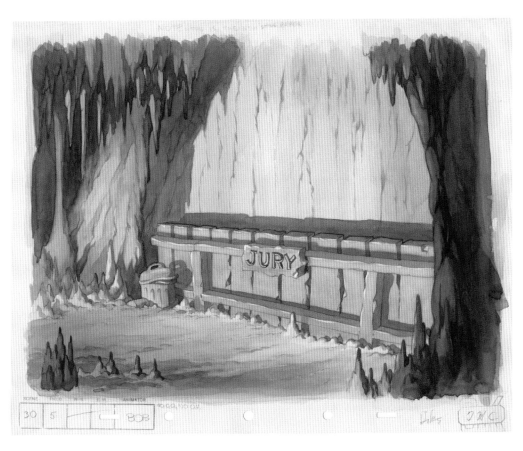

MUSIC LAND 1935

Henry
Pips US29 3 3/6 · 5/6 Reflections

COCK O' THE WALK 1935

HENS LOOKING
FROM BUILDINGS

S.31

SCENE	FIELD	N.S.	E.W.	ANIMATOR
4	5	-	-	ERIC

MICKEY'S GRAND OPERA 1936

THREE LITTLE WOLVES 1936

ELMER ELEPHANT 1936

US-33

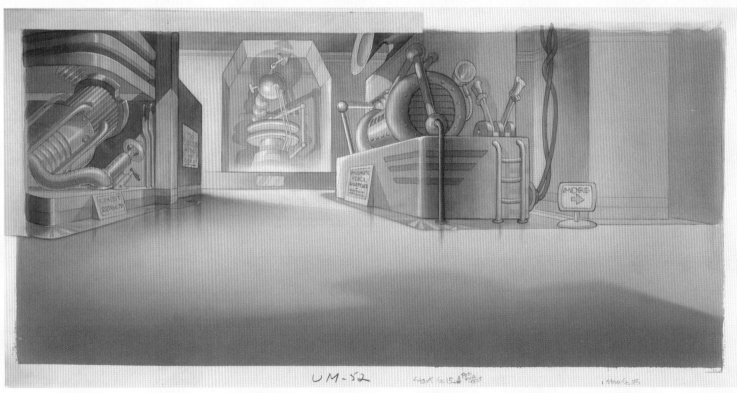

MODERN INVENTIONS 1937

SNOW WHITE AND THE SEVEN DWARFS 1937

LAYOUT & BACKGROUND

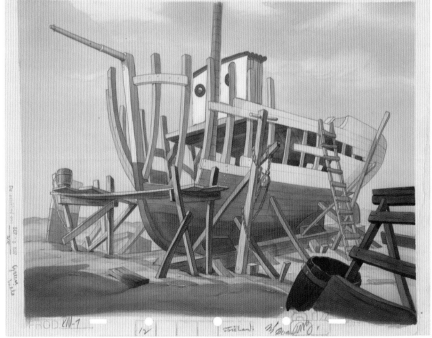

BOAT BUILDERS 1938

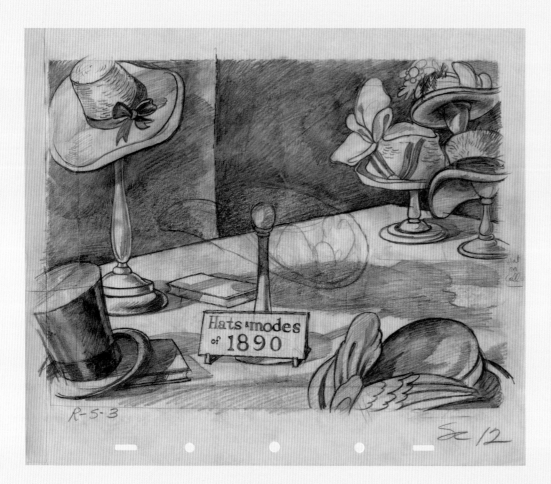

MOTH AND THE FLAME 1938

FOLLOWING SPREAD: **BRAVE LITTLE TAILOR** 1938

3 R.S. 3 - Sc. ① Sc. 1

SOCIETY DOG SHOW 1939

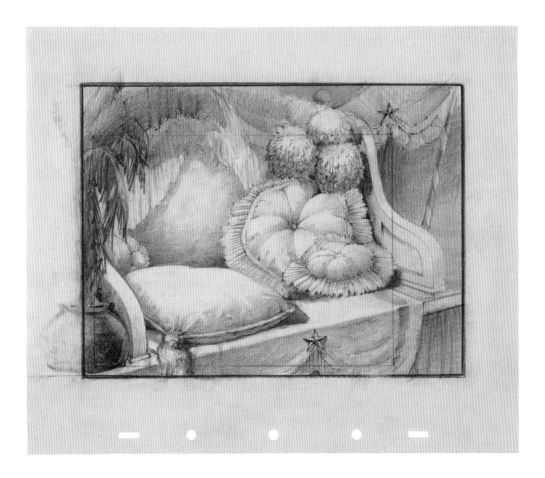

C-2

SC 21
B.6

"0 54"
SCENE 54
2242

SCENE 54
2242

MR. MOUSE TAKES A TRIP 1940

SCENE 54
2242

PINOCCHIO 1940

2003 — 1.1 — 32.1

MUSIC BOX

FANTASIA, "THE PASTORAL SYMPHONY" 1940

Puscard

F-2004
SEQ-11
SC-19

Reduce to 4F

FANTASIA, "NIGHT ON BALD MOUNTAIN" 1940

THE ART OF SKIING 1941

BIGGEST LITTLE SHOW ON EARTH

DUMBO 1941

BAMBI 1942

2002 SEQ 2.5 Sc. 13.1 BG#1 BG#2 BG-13-1A

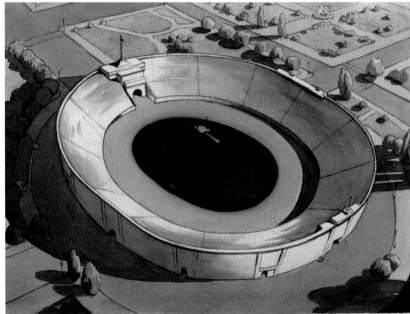

THE OLYMPIC CHAMP 1942

HOW TO SWIM 1942

THE ARMY MASCOT 1942

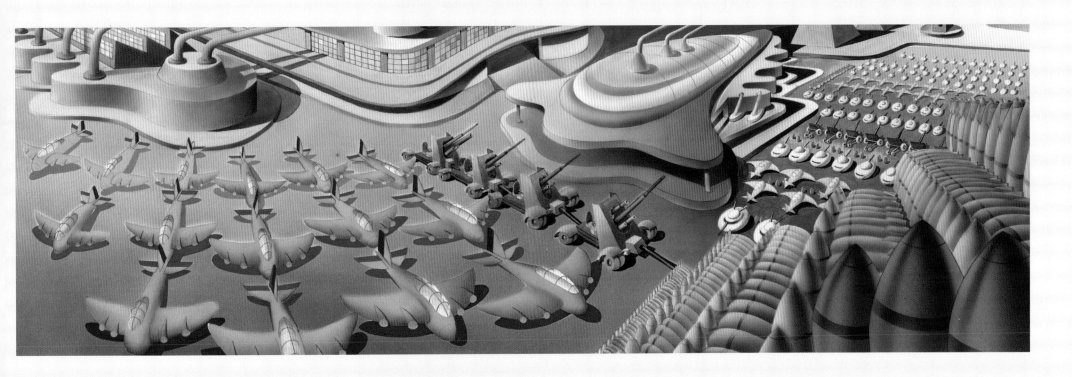

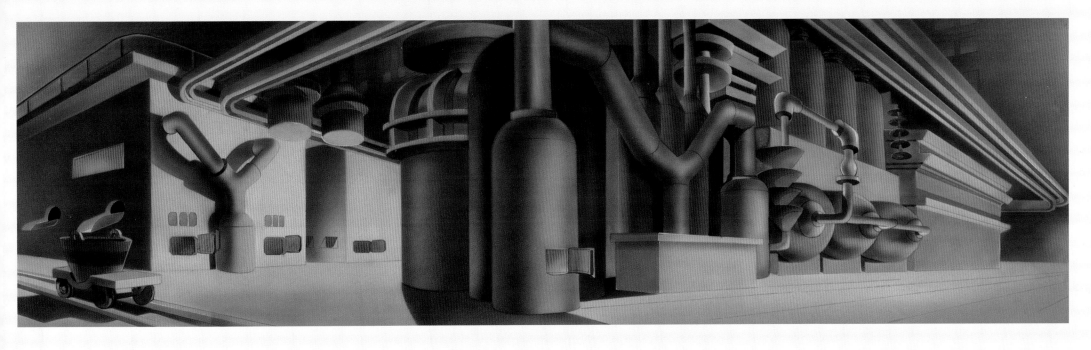

DEFENSE AGAINST INVASION 1943

VICTORY VEHICLES 1943

SC. 4
2299

FIRST AIDERS 1944

DUCK PIMPLES 1945

MAKE MINE MUSIC, "JOHNNIE FEDORA AND ALICE BLUEBONNET" 1946

old. 2046 — 1 — 63
new. 2046 - 9 - 63

SC 63 · 2046.

MELODY TIME, "JOHNNY APPLESEED" 1948

PLUTO AND THE GOPHER 1950

CINDERELLA 1950

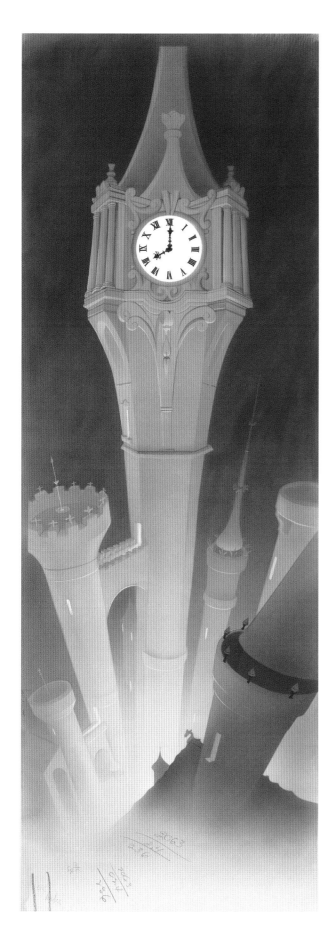

~and
they lived happily
ever after~

TRAILER HORN 1950

BEE AT THE BEACH 1950

ALICE IN WONDERLAND 1951

Ac 22.1 Seg 6 2069

SUSIE, THE LITTLE BLUE COUPE 1952

THE LITTLE HOUSE 1952

PETER PAN 1953

PIGS IS PIGS 1954

LADY AND THE TRAMP 1955

BEEZY BEAR 1955

A COWBOY NEEDS A HORSE 1956

HOW TO RELAX 1957

2479-4 2479 Sc. 4 2479

PAUL BUNYAN 1958

HOW TO HAVE AN ACCIDENT AT WORK 1959

SLEEPING BEAUTY 1959

ONE HUNDRED AND ONE DALMATIANS 1961

2110
seq 1
sc 5

start sc 5

2110—1—5

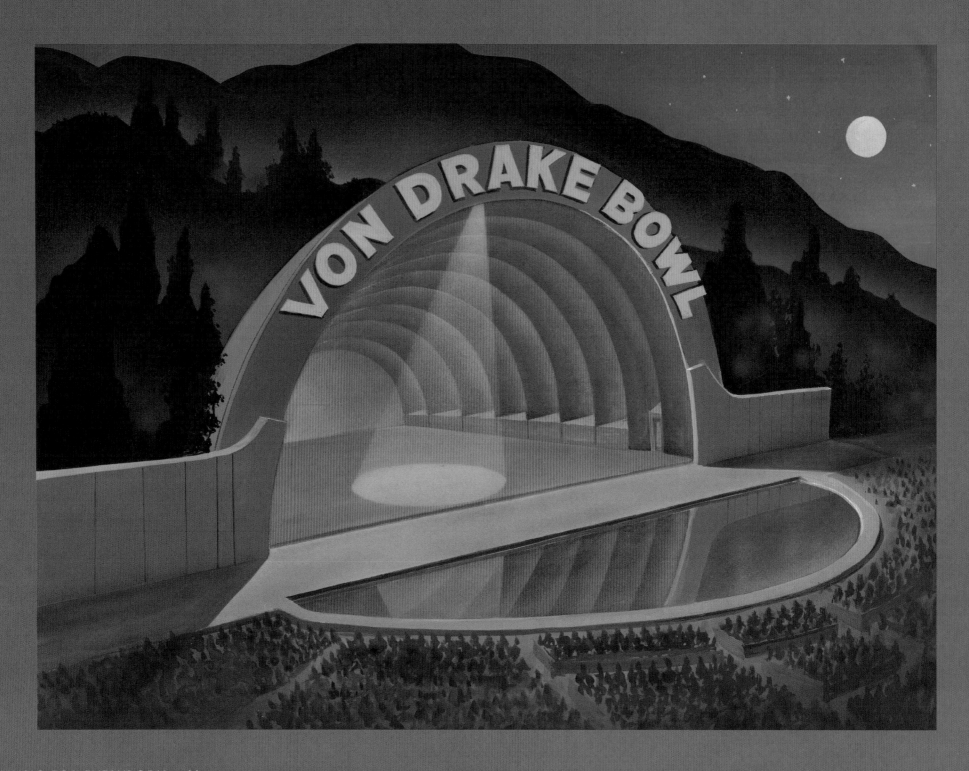

MUSIC FOR EVERYBODY 1966

THE JUNGLE BOOK 1967

MATCH TO SC. 26 SEQ. OO6
2/79

THE ARISTOCATS 1970

ROBIN HOOD 1973

THE RESCUERS 1977

THE FOX AND THE HOUND 1981

THE GREAT MOUSE DETECTIVE 1986

WHO FRAMED ROGER RABBIT 1988

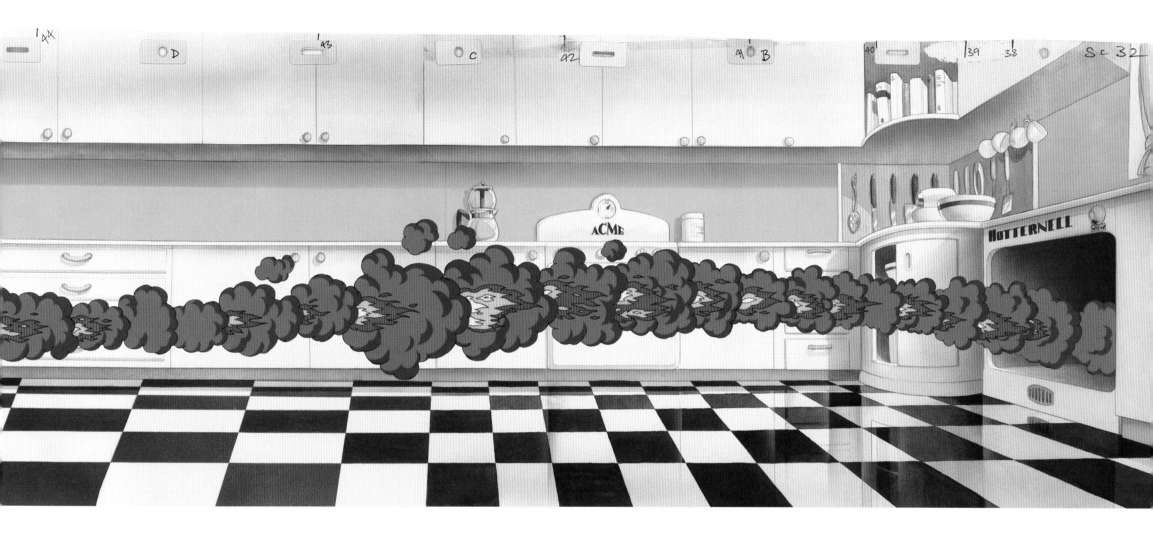

TUMMY TROUBLE 1989

OLIVER & COMPANY 1988

THE LITTLE MERMAID 1989

0497 SEQ 9.1 SC. 46

BEAUTY AND THE BEAST 1991

LAYOUT & BACKGROUND

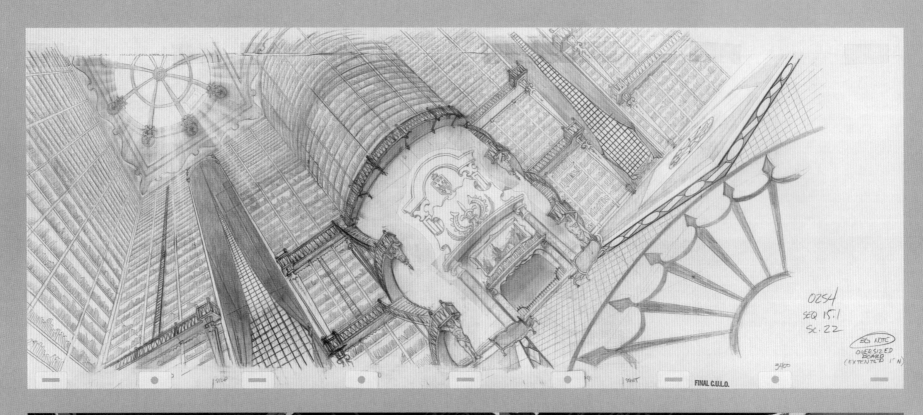

ALADDIN 1992

KEY LEVEL

FINAL C.U.L.O.

OL·UL, B-L
Sc20
SEG-20
0885

THE LION KING 1994

SQ 15.4 SAME AS UL - 1 0885 G.D.
 SC.13
 5000 FINAL C.U.L.O.

SEQ 5 SC 36 SA 42

POCAHONTAS 1995

PROD: 1446 SEQ: 14 SC: 57 IAN

THE HUNCHBACK OF NOTRE DAME 1996

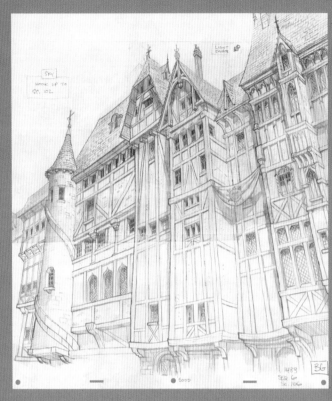

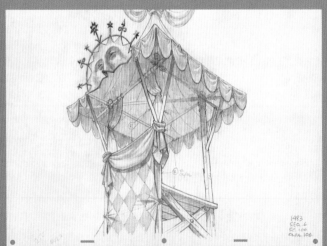

HERCULES 1997

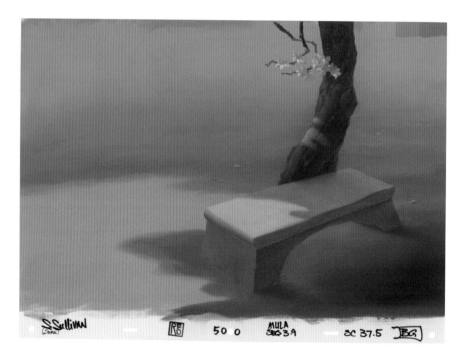

MULAN 1998

TARZ Seq. 4.6
SC. 34 BG
S/A 38

OK
MHUNT
YASUDA

FANTASIA/2000, "SYMPHONY NO. 5" 2000

- PASTELS -
224-P 245-P
275-P 234-P
285-P

BG-2
Scene 11

BEES
SEQ 2
Scene 11

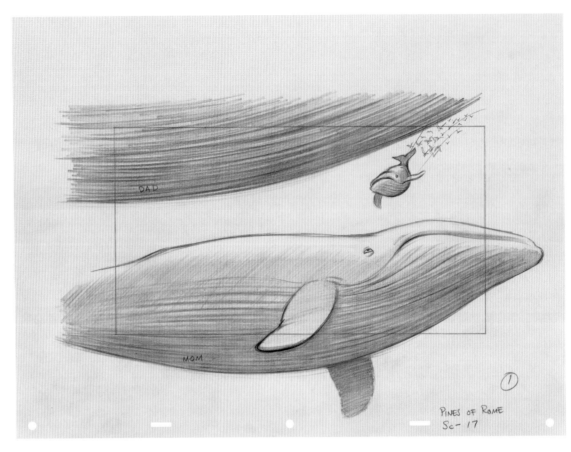

FANTASIA/2000, "PINES OF ROME" 2000

Carl Jones 0666 5000 kp SEQ 10 SC 17 BG. 17

m. G. gil

1331
GROOVE Miguel Gill SQ 1 SC 87 BG

THE EMPEROR'S NEW GROOVE 2000

232 LAYOUT & BACKGROUND

ATLANTIS: THE LOST EMPIRE 2001

LILO & STITCH 2002

THE ARCHIVE SERIES 237

c Vollmer

5000

LiLO SEQ. 12.7 SC. 68.5

WilliamSilvers · S000 · LILO · SQ26 SC64 · Photo 9

BROTHER BEAR 2003

HOME ON THE RANGE 2004

SWEA · 6/14.85 UL-3

Southside
Of Oakey
Oaks
Town Square

Hutches Private Eye Theatre Cheese Shop China Shop

CHICKEN LITTLE 2005

MEET THE ROBINSONS 2007

BOLT 2008

THE PRINCESS AND THE FROG 2009

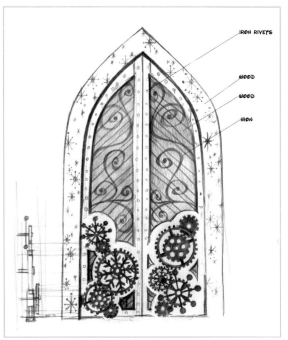

IRON RIVETS

WOOD

WOOD

IRON

PREP & LANDING 2009

TANGLED 2010

WINNIE THE POOH 2011

5561
Act III
Sc 28

FINAL STOP 9 90

ABOVE: THE GOOFY SUCCESS STORY 1955; OVERFLAP LEFT: HOW TO HOOK UP YOUR HOME THEATER 2007; OVERFLAP RIGHT: FATHERS ARE PEOPLE 1951

CLOCKWISE FROM TOP LEFT:
Al Dempster; Ralph Hulett; Joe Hale;
a group session — left to right, Dick
Lucas, Woolie Reitherman, Betsy Gossin,
John Sibley, Don Griffith, and Basil
Davidovich; Art Riley, and Walt Peregoy

CLOCKWISE FROM TOP LEFT: Doug Walker, Bill Perkins, Lisa Keene, Rasoul Azadani, David Womersley, Mac George, Sunny Apinchapong, James A. Finch, Doug Ball (middle)

ART CREDITS

FANTASIA, "THE PASTORAL SYMPHONY" 1940

INDEX

MAGIC HIGHWAY, U.S.A. 1958

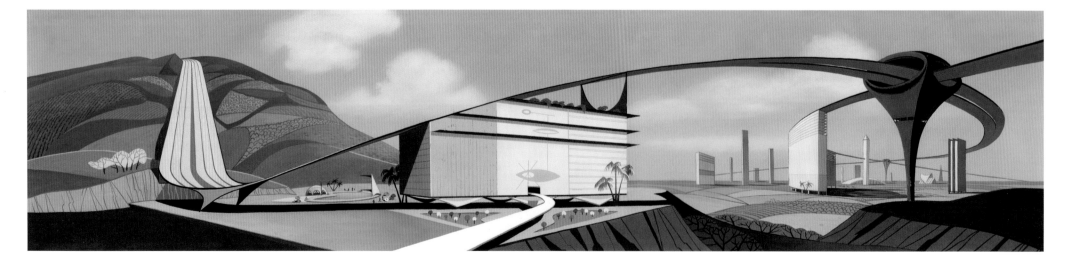

ONE HUNDRED AND ONE DALMATIANS 1961